Williamsburg:
Cradle of the First Liberty

Thomas Jefferson.

Williamsburg:
Cradle of the First Liberty

By William Lee Miller
and Cynthia M. Miller

The Colonial Williamsburg Foundation
Williamsburg, Virginia

© 1988 by The Colonial Williamsburg Foundation

All rights reserved, including the right to reproduce this book or portions thereof in any form.

Printed in the United States of America

ISBN 0-87935-078-4

COVER—*The Raleigh Tavern was the center of social, political, and business activities in eighteenth-century Williamsburg. Patriots met here to voice their opposition to the policies of the British crown. Along with the formal sessions at the Capitol, other important meetings at the Raleigh foreshadowed American independence and the U.S. Constitution. The ideas of liberty, a union of the thirteen colonies, freedom of religion, speech, press, and other freedoms cherished today were discussed in the Raleigh.*

Foreword

VISITORS come to Colonial Williamsburg for a variety of purposes, and frequently discover entirely new reasons that cause them to return again and again. The physical beauty of the town itself; the relaxed ambience; the style of the surviving buildings and craftsmanship of others authentically reconstructed; the excellence of the interpretive staff including the skilled tradesmen and women; the openness of the greens and loveliness of the gardens—each facet contributes to a memorable whole.

The most significant reason of all, however, is the intellectual legacy of the eighteenth century, the ideas that were conceived, debated, and put into action here that helped shape our country. These ideas, expounded in Williamsburg by Virginians and then in Philadelphia by leaders from all the colonies, have proved themselves enduringly sound and a source of inspiration for millions of Americans and, over time, for millions more on every continent of the globe.

The most fundamental of these ideas, and the most distinctively American, is the concept of freedom of religion. Article XVI of George Mason's Virginia Declaration of Rights, adopted in Williamsburg on June 12, 1776, is an important milestone on the road to religious liberty. For the first time, the words "free exercise," originally proposed by James Madison, replaced the softer notion of tolerance: "All Men are equally entitled to the free Exercise of Religion, according to the Dictates of Conscience."

Three years later, Thomas Jefferson's Bill for Religious Freedom was also introduced at the Capitol in Williamsburg, but, because it was too controversial for enaction at the time, it was tabled. Only after years of debate and the trials of a War for Independence was a revised statute passed in 1786 by the Virginia General Assembly. Its enactment was due largely to the brilliant scholarship, dogged persistence, and political genius of James Madison.

The essence of this bill eventually became a foundation stone for the First Amendment to the United States Constitution. Jefferson considered the Virginia Statute for Religious Freedom important enough to be listed as one of his three chief accomplishments on his gravestone, along with the Declaration of Independence and the University of Virginia. As Jefferson wrote in the preamble of his bill, "Truth is great and will prevail . . . Almighty God hath created the mind free."

Colonial Williamsburg is grateful to the Williamsburg Charter Foundation for conceiving and organizing the "First Liberty" Summit as a means of celebrating religious freedom and the First Amendment. We are grateful also to Mutual of America, and to their chairman, Mr. William J. Flynn, for underwriting the several special events of the "First Liberty" Summit on June 24–26, 1988, and the publication of this essay.

Charles R. Longsworth

Williamsburg has a prominent place in the history of religious liberty, not because of any dramatic action on the battlefield, or any decision in the legislative chambers, or any other kind of outward happening, but because of the stirrings that took place here within the human mind.

Ideas that developed here worked their way into the fabric of the Commonwealth of Virginia, of the United States of America, and of the subsequent history of liberty worldwide.

The College of William and Mary—Wren Building

In March 1760 young Thomas Jefferson arrived here at this college for Virginia gentlemen, then the only college in Virginia and one of only six in the colonies. He came from the west—the Virginia Piedmont, almost to the Blue Ridge Mountains, at Shadwell. What this young man was to learn in Williamsburg would affect the lives of all who would one day be Americans, and on no subject more than what he would call freedom of the human mind.

Thomas Jefferson was a student in the College of William and Mary in his sixteenth, seventeenth, and eighteenth years, from March 1760 until April 1762. He then took up the study of law, also in Williamsburg, with George Wythe, in his nineteenth through his twenty-fourth years. In other words, Jefferson spent

The Sir Christopher Wren Building of the College of William and Mary.

his formative years at this college and in this town. He was a student and an active reader and thinker all his life, of course, but the years at the beginning of his adult life, when he could spend all his time studying and thinking and forming his ideas, were spent here in Williamsburg.

Jefferson's most important teacher at the College of William and Mary was a man named William Small. Small was the professor of natural philosophy (mathematics, and also physics and metaphysics) who, because of an upheaval at the college, also came to teach Jefferson moral philosophy: rhetoric, ethics, and literature.

Small was the only layman among the seven faculty members then teaching at the Anglican college (as William and Mary then was) and, in Jefferson's opinion, certainly the ablest of the group. He was a Scot, who would eventually return to the British Isles. The Scottish universities at that period were the center of an intellectual ferment. Listening to Small on their walks around Williamsburg, Jefferson was introduced to the ideas of this exceptional group of professors at Edinburgh and Glasgow—to the Scottish Enlightenment. Jefferson learned substantial lessons about the new worlds of science, and about the significance of the outlook of the new philosophers of the Enlightenment in Europe.

In the autobiography he wrote as an old man, Thomas Jefferson recalled what William Small had meant to him:

> *It was my great good fortune, and what probably fixed the destinies of my life, that Dr. William Small of Scotland was then professor of Mathematics, a man profound in the most useful branches of science, with a happy talent of communication, correct and gentlemanly manners, and an enlarged and liberal mind. He, most happily for me, became soon attached to me, and made me his daily companion when not engaged in the school; and from his conversation I got my first views of the expansion of science, and of the system of things in which we are placed.*

George Wythe House

On completing his college work, just after his nineteenth birthday, Jefferson proceeded to the study of law, also in Williamsburg. His teacher was George Wythe, another able representative of the intellectual tides of the time. During the four years Jefferson studied law, he probably lived at the Market Square Tavern and walked every day past the Magazine, around the corner by Bruton Parish Church, toward the Governor's Palace, to be greeted by a "middle-sized, hook-nosed gentleman," the inhabitant of the Wythe House.

Wythe was about thirty-five years old in 1762, when Jefferson began studying with him, and was an eminent member of the bar. An English traveler, not much impressed with most of the colonials he met, said that Wythe at the time had a "perfect knowledge" of Greek and ancient philosophy. Moreover, said the traveler, Wythe was a man of "such a profound reverence for the Supreme Being, such respect for the divine law, such philanthropy for mankind, such simplicity of manners, and such inflexible rectitude and integrity of principle, as would have dignified a Roman Senator . . ."

Over the half-century of his public career, Wythe was not only Virginia's—and the colonies'—first professor of law, but also a member of the House of Burgesses, Virginia's first signer of the Declaration of Independence, one of the framers of the Constitution, a judge, and mayor of Williamsburg. He was educated by his Quaker mother and shared many of the advanced concerns of enlightened folk of that day: care of the insane; the inclusion of science in the college curriculum; and fair treatment for Indians and blacks (he freed several of his slaves, provided for others in his will, and taught several of them to read and write Greek as well as English). Though he was a member of the Bruton Parish vestry, he had independent views on the established Anglican church. He was a partisan not only of religious liberty but also of an idea that went further: separation of church and state. He was an advocate of freedom of thought and speech. Wythe had a substantial influence on Jefferson, who called him "my most affectionate friend through life."

The Governor's Palace

The third person to have a noteworthy effect on Thomas Jefferson during his years as a student in Williamsburg was the lieutenant governor, Francis Fauquier. Fauquier was a man of

The Governor's Palace.

culture and wide learning, well known for his scientific and humanitarian concerns, who was a popular and well respected governor. Virginians would name a county for him (thereby saddling their English-speaking descendants with the problem of trying to pronounce his name—FAW-keer).

Fauquier's curiosity about the natural world may well have influenced young Jefferson. His observations in 1758 about hailstones, summarized in the Royal Society's *Philosophical Transactions*, were of the exacting and detailed sort for which Jefferson later was to become known. Fauquier was also practical: he used the hailstones he gathered for study to cool wine and freeze ice cream.

Like Wythe, Fauquier had rather loose ties to the established Anglican church. He was not convinced of Christ's divinity and tried to persuade the rector of Bruton Parish Church to strike the Apostles' Creed from the liturgy. He believed Voltaire's popular saying, "much to be pitied are they who need the help of religion to be honest men," and this idea, separating morality from religion, influenced Jefferson.

Fauquier brought other modern attitudes to Williamsburg. For example, he promoted the establishment of a hospital for "Persons who are so unhappy as to be deprived of their reason." In colonial Virginia the care of the mentally ill was left to the vestry of each parish. If the vestry was unable to provide such care, the insane were either left at large in a world with which they could not cope, or, if unruly, jailed. Taking this charge away from the church, Fauquier urged the General Assembly to "make Provision for the Support and Maintenance of Ideots, Lunaticks, and other Persons of unsound Minds." Williamsburg's Public Hospital, which opened in 1773, was the earliest facility in North America devoted entirely to the care and treatment of the mentally ill.

Young Jefferson visited the Governor's Palace regularly. He played his violin with other amateurs in the ballroom, walked in the luxurious gardens, or dined while discussing politics, literature, the troubles at the college, and changes at the church with Fauquier, Wythe, and Small. Not every governor—not every professor—would be so enlightened as to include such a young man, however bright, in his social conversations, but these men did. These three were a lesser trinity bearing the message of the Enlightenment from the greater trinity who were to be Jefferson's heroes throughout his life: John Locke, Isaac Newton, and Francis Bacon.

Bruton Parish Church

But the rest of the world did not necessarily look upon religious issues in the way they were talked about at Fauquier's table and in Small's classroom. When young Thomas Jefferson studied in Williamsburg, established churches and the ideas that supported them were still the pattern throughout Christendom. So it had been in the history of Europe for fourteen hundred years—since Emperor Constantine raised the cross as the insignia of the Roman Legions and made Christianity the official religion of the late Roman Empire. So it was throughout the Catholic ages, with the universal church claiming the support of temporal power. So it continued to be after the Protestant Reformation. The several branches of Protestant Christianity—Anglican in England; Lutheran in the Scandinavian countries and Germany; Reformed or "Calvinist" in Switzerland, Holland, Scotland, and other lands—now linked the national governments each to its own form of the Christian religion. Theologians of all varieties thought that there must be a unity of the people's temporal and spiritual allegiances and that there was a clear Christian truth that the state ought to recognize and support. But they disagreed, country by country, as to the form of that Christian truth.

In the sixteenth and seventeenth centuries a few voices on the fringes, particularly in the ferment surrounding the Puritan Revolution in seventeenth-century England, began to question the ideas that church and state had to be linked, and that Christian truth should use the temporal power of the state. Roger Williams—whom we will meet again farther along in these pages—sharply attacked the "Bloody Tenant" of "persecution for cause of conscience . . . ," that is, for religious belief. Williams and some others began to point out that it was a little paradoxical to cut people's ears off and burn them to death in the name of the religion of love.

The little band of Pilgrims who came to the place in New England they called Plimoth Plantation in 1620 were part of the ferment that would one day lead to a different relationship of religion to society. They were "Separatists," that is, they could find no Biblical justification for the Church of England, and they separated from it, a shocking step at the time, because it was a violation of the laws of the state—something like treason—as well as of the church, because state and church, king and bishop, were tied together.

The much larger body of Puritans who came a dozen years later on the *Arbella* and her sister ships to Massachusetts Bay were *not* Separatists, although it was convenient for them to have the de facto separation from the English church provided by the Atlantic Ocean. They believed in their own way in a national

Bruton Parish Church.

church, a purified version of the Church of England, and in the use of the temporal power for religious ends, not as it was done in London, with the unbiblical bishops and Romish practices, but as it was done in Boston, in the Congregational and—as they saw it—truly Biblical way.

But in many countries there was beginning to be within Protestant Christianity itself a growing challenge to the idea of the state church, and to persecution for religious reasons, from Quakers and Seekers and Baptists and Anabaptists and Mennonites and many other sectarian groups, and from individual religious thinkers. The New World across the Atlantic was thought to be a haven, an asylum, and a new start for these better ideas, not only to build one's own unitary religious commonwealth—a city on a hill—as in New England, but also to live in peace with many other religions, as in Pennsylvania. These worldwide religious impulses combined with the impulses from the Enlightenment—from people like Small and Wythe and the people they read in Europe—to break this centuries-old pattern of the union of church and state, and of the use of state power to enforce religious belief.

The place where that would be decisively broken in a lasting way was here in Virginia, and the leader of the successful effort that broke that system was the sometime student at William and Mary, Thomas Jefferson.

When Jefferson studied in Williamsburg, the old model still prevailed. The Church of England, part of the worldwide pattern of established churches, had long ago come to Virginia as part of the first settlers' English heritage—they were Englishmen, and the English church came with them and the royal charter to this English colony. The church was woven into the fabric of life and of government. According to its dissenting critics, the Anglican church of eighteenth-century Virginia was not the center of a vibrant religion, but rather more of a social institution, with some priests given to rum and horses, and with automatic connections to the ruling families: it was a social–religious amalgam that reinforced the prevailing order. It is hard for Americans two hundred years later to believe that there was a time when in a colony like Virginia the church was an arm of the government somewhat like our public highway department, but by law it was, loosely, something like that.

One can see the close relationship between church and state, and perhaps between church and the society's pattern of hierar-

The governor sat in the canopied chair; members of his Council and visiting dignitaries filled the seats next to him.

chy and dominance, in Bruton Parish Church itself. Near the chancel at the front of the church there is the thronelike governor's chair, canopied and embellished. With the governor sat the members of his Council and occasionally visiting dignitaries; behind them, in the space reserved for the choir these days, sat the twelve members of the vestry. The twelve vestrymen of Bruton Parish, like vestrymen everywhere in Virginia—including the plantation-owning fathers of both Thomas Jefferson and James Madison—were chosen not for piety and religious devotion but for social position, and were concerned with the upkeep of roads and care of the poor and sick, as well as the maintenance of the church.

Social position and government were woven into the church; religion was woven into government. The House of Burgesses conducted a prayer service before each session. The legislators had a committee on religion, and discussed regulations having to do with the pay of clergy and, under certain circumstances, even matters of doctrine.

There were no civil officials to record births or deaths, so the only way to register a birth was to have the child baptized in the Anglican church. This meant that practically everybody was at least nominally Anglican. Only Anglican ministers could conduct marriages. The state regulated attendance at local parishes; if a citizen neglected to go to church, he could be fined, or put in the pillory or stocks. (This law was enforced unevenly: if the miller missed services on a day the wind was blowing, no fine was required of him.) All working subjects, regardless of religious preference, were required to support their local parish of the Church of England with their taxes. (To be sure, as we suggested above, the church did play a role—caring for the poor, orphans, and the like—that would later be assigned to other institutions.)

The Anglican church in late eighteenth-century Virginia was, according to some, not a particularly vigorous or energetic religious institution. It was thoroughly accommodated, as the New Lights would put it, to "the World," ripe for reform and vulnerable to attack. Which came.

Virginia's Importance for Religious Liberty

Williamsburg was the center of events in Virginia during the Revolutionary era, and Virginia in turn was an important center

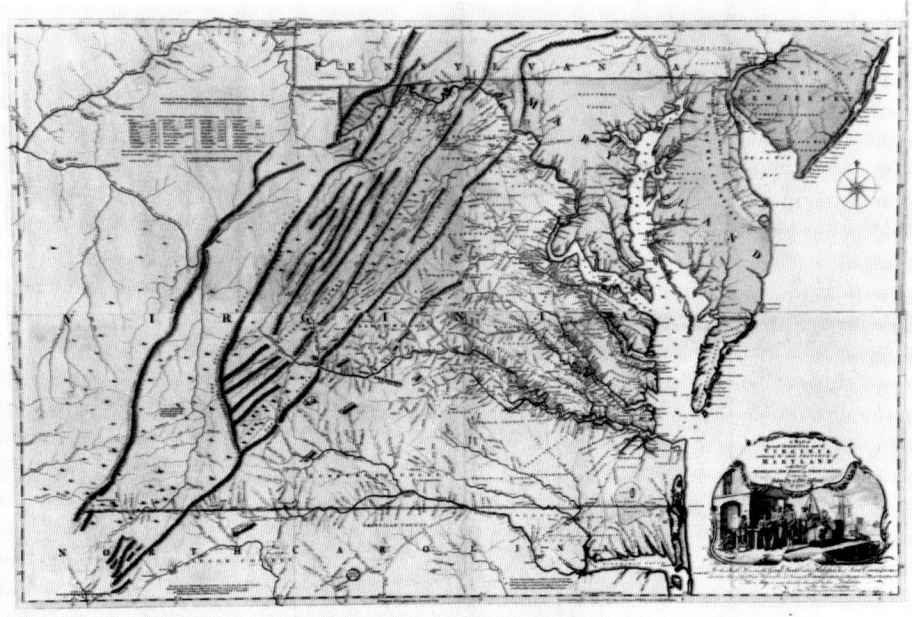

"A map of the most inhabited part of Virginia" drawn in 1751 by Joshua Fry and Peter Jefferson, father of Thomas Jefferson.

of development of the American tradition of religious liberty. It had that central place for four reasons:

1. It was the largest of the thirteen colonies;

2. It included in its population able and numerous supporters of both sides of the controversy over church and state—not only eminent Anglican conservative gentlemen here in Williamsburg, but numerous Presbyterian, Baptist, and other dissenters farther west;

3. The change in religious policy that took place in Virginia was the most radical of all state changes and influenced the others;

4. The leaders who contributed to these changes became policymakers for the United States as a whole.

The Dissenters

Along with the established government-supported church, Virginia—as we have said—had a large and growing number of people who were not Anglicans—who were "dissenters" from the established church.

Of course members of an established church in one place could be "dissenters" in another—Anglicans were "dissenters" in this sense in Connecticut and Massachusetts, with their Puritan Congregational establishments. Some of the dissenters in Virginia were immigrants who brought a religion other than Anglicanism with them—the Scotch-Irish Presbyterians in the Shenandoah Valley, who had come down from Pennsylvania, were perhaps the most numerous and important—and they might well have been supporters of the established Scottish church back in Scotland. The same might be said of the German Lutherans in Fredericksburg and in the Valley. There was also in Virginia at that time a sprinkling of Quakers, a sprinkling of Jews, a sprinkling of others who came by their "dissenting" or non-Anglican religious position by inheritance, as it were.

But in addition to those groups there were the products of the revivals—much more disturbing to the old Anglican order. In the 1730s and 1740s there had been a torrent of religious revivals across all the colonies—called the Great Awakening—that left many pools of new believers in the Virginia Piedmont and elsewhere. (Coming from God as the rains from heaven is the way many of the leaders of the Great Awakening saw these astonishing revivals.) The earliest wave of these "New Lights"—as the "born again" converts in the revivals were also called—were Presbyterians who formed the famous Hanover Presbytery concentrated around Richmond in what is today central Virginia. They were followed in the middle of the century by a more numerous and, from the point of view of the old Anglicans, more outlandish group of converts, the Separate Baptists, concentrated farther west. It was the arrest of some of these Separate Baptist preachers, some of whom continued to preach even from jail, that outraged young James Madison and first engaged him in the great issues of the Revolution. Still later in the eighteenth century there would come within the Anglican church itself a movement of "Methodists," imported of course from England, which was also a product of the revivalism of the time.

These converts from the revivals were particularly disturbing to the old Anglican establishment because they did not come to their religious belief by birthright, as a gentleman ought to do, nor did their preachers stay put in one parish, giving sober and learned sermons reinforcing the social order, as a gentleman's pastor ought to do. The New Lights came to their religious belief by adult conversion. The eighteenth-century word, originally derisive, for them was "Enthusiasts." The preachers these enthusiasts went to hear often were traveling evangelists, the greatest of whom was an Englishman named George Whitefield, whose travels across the American colonies made him perhaps the first American celebrity. Whitefield preached at Bruton Parish Church in Williamsburg on December 16, 1739. These New Light converts grew at an alarming rate, from the point of view of the old establishment.

Combining all of the non-Anglican citizens in Virginia, both New Lights and others, made a formidable group.

Thomas Jefferson was to write:

By the time of the Revolution two thirds of Virginia's population were dissenters.

If we look beyond Virginia, we see that dissenting Protestantism—that is, Puritan Protestantism and Sectarian Protestantism—provided much of the support for religious liberty and the independence of the church from the state in the other colonies on the American shores, in England, and throughout the Christian world. Although the main body of English Puritans was not tolerant, in the excited argumentation of the Puritan Civil War in seventeenth-century England some persons and movements on the radical edge of the movement did argue for a religious and intellectual toleration, and for a time the Puritan Commonwealth had a religious toleration beyond anything England had theretofore experienced.

The English Puritan movement, as we have said, spilled across the Atlantic in the fabled Pilgrims of 1620, a small band of Separatists who came to Plymouth, and then in the much larger Massachusetts Bay area, where they intended to establish a truly Christian commonwealth, a city on a hill to all the world. Although they did not welcome religious diversity—quite the contrary—the movement of which they were a part generated ideas that led in that direction. Out of the center of Puritanism both in England and in the United States there came movements and thinkers who would reject the idea of persecution for reasons of religion: Quakers like William Penn, many Baptists, Seekers, Levelers, Independents.

It is important to understand that several voices and movements both in the American colonies and in England itself in the seventeenth century defended religious toleration not on the grounds of indifference or rationalism but on the grounds of the Christian Gospel . . . not *in spite* of their religious belief, but because of it. John Milton is the best known of many in England; Roger Williams in Rhode Island is perhaps the greatest of all. For him, respecting another human being's conscience did not mean that he held less firmly to the religious truths that he himself believed but rather that those religious truths in which he believed required him to respect the consciences of all others—even, astonishingly in his time and place, the consciences of "Papists"!

But the position that these visionaries took in the middle of the seventeenth century was not to prevail as the policy of the state—except for the little colony of Rhode Island and Providence Plantations in the New World—until late in the eighteenth century. Really, it was not to be enacted into the formal law of a major political unit until the Virginia Assembly passed Jefferson's statute for religious freedom in 1786.

That would come about by the rather curious combination of two somewhat oddly joined forces: the Enlightenment thinkers, like Jefferson and his teachers and their teachers, who furnished most of the intellectual leadership, and the pietists, revivalists, and evangelicals, who furnished most of the votes and popular support and the added passion.

The Capitol . . . the General Assembly . . . Spring 1776

The story in Virginia begins in the immensely important year of 1776. In May of that year the gentlemen of Virginia passed a resolution for the colony's total separation from England. Much excitement had preceded this resolution: in 1765 in Williamsburg in the House of Burgesses Patrick Henry's voice had rung out against the Stamp Tax; later the House of Burgesses created a day of fasting and prayer at Bruton Parish Church in support of their Boston compatriots' dealings with the tea; in Richmond still later another of Mr. Henry's speeches so impressed members of the loosely organized, growing militia that they rushed out to have "Liberty or Death" printed on the hunting shirts that they would wear to war.

In the spring of 1775 Governor Dunmore had removed the gunpowder from the Magazine at Williamsburg and fled the Palace. Hiding on a warship off the coast, he directed the ship to fire on Norfolk on January 1, 1776. Later that same day, colonial troops added to the conflagration by setting fire to houses not hit by the ship's guns. Ardent Virginia patriots hoisted a new flag over the Capitol weeks before the resolution for independence

George Wythe.

was accepted by the Continental Congress in Philadelphia. Now, in the muggy heat of a Williamsburg spring, a group of men gathered at the Capitol not only to carry out this mission by declaring Virginia's independence but also to create the structure of a new government.

The Virginians took a portentous first step in the forming of that government: they formulated a declaration of what we would today call "human rights." This document, the Virginia Declaration of Rights, was drafted by a man named George Mason, who is little known by Americans today but ought to be better known. A self-educated plantation owner from the Northern Neck and an elder statesman, Mason had a sharp legal mind and more knowledge of human rights, colonial charters, and proper constitutions than anyone in the colony. Suffering from the gout and uncomfortable in the taverns of Williamsburg, he used his law books and probably the libraries of George Wythe and the College of William and Mary to put together his Declaration.

This document, only a few hundred words long, simply announces man's native freedom from restraint and clarifies his basic rights. But these ideas of freedom and equality heralded a new age, when man's rights and liberties would form the basis of government. The Virginia Declaration of Rights, adopted in early June 1776, was the first in a long and important sequence of which the federal Bill of Rights is a part; it influenced other

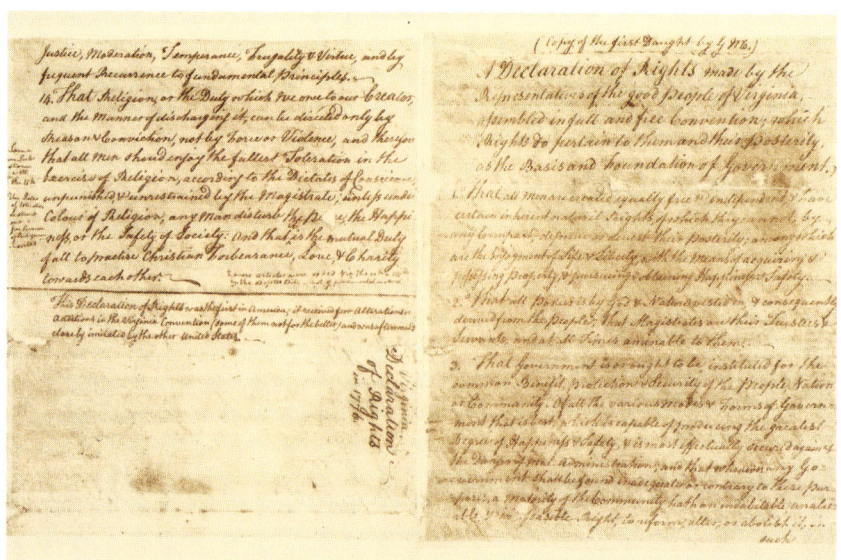

A copy of the first draft of the Virginia Declaration of Rights, in George Wythe's hand.

colonies and eventually other countries. Jefferson surely was thinking of it as he wrote the Declaration of Independence a month or so later.

In general there were few grumbles from the benches as the statesmen discussed the Virginia Declaration of Rights. Some compromise was needed to modify Mason's statement that "all men are created equal," but that immensely significant issue, in all its potent meaning, could not be faced and was papered over in slaveholding Virginia.

But on another matter, religion, there was some dispute. Mason was a conventional Anglican and he wrote what most of the delegates probably thought to be a quite adequate statement:

All men should enjoy the fullest toleration of the exercise of religion according to the dictates of conscience.

What was wrong with that? It echoed the opinions of good republicans following upon John Locke's letter concerning toleration and the English act of toleration of the previous century.

But for one young man sitting there in Williamsburg that was not enough. This was the youthful delegate from Orange County, James Madison, Jr., who was making his first appearance in the great world of public affairs. He was shy and short and new and diffident and his voice was weak and he did not play a visible role in this Williamsburg Convention, but nevertheless he was not going to let mere "toleration" carry the day.

We may guess that the very word gave him intellectual heartburn. He had been to college up north at the College of New Jersey where in the excited, revolutionary, whiggish atmosphere the young men and their teachers had lively debates about revolutionary political and religious ideas.

One of these ideas was that mere "toleration," which implied condescension—which implied there was some institution or belief in a superior position from which to do the tolerating—was not enough.

These young patriots of the Revolution were moving on to the position that every man's conscience was equal in its rights to every other man's and that the state had no role in determining which one was better.

So in Williamsburg not too long after he left Princeton young James (Jemmy) Madison asked an older and more distinguished delegate to offer an amendment to the proposed Declaration of Rights.

The Capitol.

He didn't get everything he wanted, but he did get the Declaration of Rights revised, with the word "toleration" struck from it so that as enacted it said that every man had an equal right to **"free exercise"** of religion. When the new Declaration of Rights was publicized throughout the colony—now the independent Commonwealth—of Virginia it aroused a response that the mostly Anglican gentry who passed it probably had not expected. The Baptists in Culpeper, the Presbyterians in the Shenandoah Valley, and the other dissenters and minority religious groups took what it said seriously—in effect—that their religious rights were *equal* to those of the members of the Church of England who had for so long dominated, by law, the affairs of the colony. These dissenters expressed their enthusiastic desire for equality in the religious realm by flooding the House of Burgesses—now called the House of Delegates—with petitions, editorials, sermons, and even poems demanding the abolition of old restrictions and impediments on their worship and life because of religion and insisting that they no longer be required to pay taxes to support a church they did not attend or believe in. This startling flood of responses was an important cause of the events that followed.

Printer–Bookbinder and Post Office—The Virginia Gazette

The Virginia Declaration of Rights, published in the *Virginia Gazette,* was read up and down the Atlantic seaboard as copies of the *Gazette* spread north and south in the saddlebags of postriders or the pouches of sea captains. In Williamsburg the Declaration was discussed over cider and beer at the Raleigh Tavern.

There was much debate in the *Gazette* over (Madison's) Article 16 concerning "free exercise of religion." Just after the Declaration of Rights was published, a dissenter calling himself a "Country Poet" wrote to the paper to celebrate his new religious equality:

> *Tax all things, water, air, and light*
> *If need there is; yea, tax the night!*
> *But let our brave heroic minds*
> *Move freely, like celestial winds.*
> *Make vice and folly feel your rod,*
> *But leave our consciences to God.*

A "Preacher of the Gospel" agreed with the Country Poet. He denounced the established Anglican preachers as "dumb dogs" and "drones, who have long lived on the sweets of the land, unprofitable to, and a heavy charge on, the public." He suggested sending all those "carnal bishops" off to fight the British, while he and others like him—Baptist and Methodist preachers—took over the Anglican churches.

The Anglicans spoke their minds in the *Gazette,* too. "Philoepiscopus" answered the Preacher of the Gospel by denouncing the "nonsense and blasphemy" of preachers who attacked the established church. They were "cheats and enthusiasts, a scandal to religion, and dangerous to the commonwealth; they break violently into the sheepfold, and stand upon record in the book of God as hirelings, thieves and robbers." This writer predicted "a civil war amongst ourselves," which he thought might be "a little unseasonable" since it looked like a war with the British was at hand.

The Capitol . . . the General Assembly . . . Fall 1776

One of those who was much stimulated by this year of Revolutionary excitement was the young product of William and Mary, Thomas Jefferson, now in his early thirties. While Mason and Madison were in Williamsburg helping to form independent Virginia's new government, Jefferson had been otherwise occupied: he had gone to Philadelphia as one of the Virginia delegates to the convention that declared the independence of all thirteen colonies. He already had a reputation as a writer, and therefore was asked by the convention to undertake the most important piece of draftsmanship in the country's history. In part he wrote:

> *We hold these truths to be self-evident, that all men are created equal, that they are endowed by their Creator with certain inalienable rights, that among these are Life, Liberty and the pursuit of Happiness.*

Jefferson then returned to what he would still regard as home country—Virginia—to try to remake it in line with the principles to which he had given immortal expression in Philadelphia. He was elected to the General Assembly for the fall of

1776 and came to Williamsburg to sit with his fellow legislators in a most important session—the first after Virginia's independence. High on the list of matters that needed to be radically revised, in his opinion, was religious policy. Jefferson rarely spoke in large gatherings, but he did speak to the General Assembly about the laws of the commonwealth dealing with religion.

> *Heresy is a capital offense, the denial of the Trinity or the divine authority of the scriptures is punishable by imprisonment, profanity is a crime, Roman Catholics are excluded from civil office, free thinkers and Unitarians are subject to be declared unfit and even having their children taken away from them.*

A supporter of the established church and a distinguished member of the old Virginia aristocracy and of the Virginia Assembly named Edmund Pendleton (whose gravestone is in the Bruton Parish churchyard, near Fauquier's) remarked that his friend Jefferson seemed to have scratched back through British and Virginia law to find every antique horror he could, old laws that were on the books but now never enforced. But Jefferson responded that enforced or not, they should be taken off the books.

Cleaning up old horrors in the law was only a small part of Jefferson's larger purpose. He wanted to create a new policy about religion and freedom of the mind for Virginia.

Jefferson had many other projects for reform, and proposed a revising of the entire legal code of the Commonwealth of Virginia from top to bottom. As often happens when you propose something, he was appointed chairman of the committee to do the revising. Edmund Pendleton and Jefferson's old teacher George Wythe were also on the committee. For months the committee members worked on this revision.

Jefferson's Great Bill—Monticello 1777

Sometime in 1777, probably sitting at his desk in Monticello, probably with John Locke's *Letter Concerning Toleration* on the table beside him and perhaps John Milton's great libertarian pamphlet *The Areopagitica* also, Jefferson composed the most important part of that revision of the laws, a bill establishing the freedom of religion.

Jefferson began his long and eloquent preamble to this bill by asserting the freedom of the human mind. He used a phrase that the Assembly's editing would eventually place at the very start and that would ring down through history:

Almighty God hath created the mind free.

By combining the freedom of the human mind—a concept most characteristic of Jefferson and the great deists of the Enlightenment—with the concept that it was almighty God who created it so—more characteristic of the dissenting Protestants and Puritans of the American colonies—Jefferson created a symbol of the two primary movements, making for a remarkable result: full religious liberty.

Jefferson had some stinging things to say about the effort to enforce religious belief by coercion:

All attempts to influence the mind by temporal punishments or burdens or by civil incapacitations tend only to beget habits of hypocrisy and meanness.

He condemned all use of compulsion to finance religion:

To compel a man to furnish money for the propagation of opinions which he disbelieves and abhors is sinful and tyrannical.

Jefferson did not want force—the power of the state—used even to raise money for one's own church:

Even the forcing of a man to support this or that teacher of his own religious persuasion is depriving him of the comfortable liberty of giving his contributions to the particular pastor whose morals he would make his pattern.

A person's religious beliefs ought not to affect in any way, favorably or unfavorably, his or her standing in the civil society:

Our civil rights have no dependence on our religious opinions, any more than our opinions in physics or geometry.

The core of Jefferson's opinion had to do with the proper relation of opinion to government:

The opinions of men are not the object of civil government, nor under its jurisdiction.

That sentence was too strong for the Virginia Assembly; they cut it out of the law as enacted.

What about religions that are dangerous to society? Jefferson gave an answer that the Supreme Court later picked up:

It is time enough for the rightful purposes of civil government for its officers to interfere when principles break out into overt acts against peace and good order.

The preamble to Jefferson's bill ended with a great passage which is central to the nation he did so much to found. It echoes Locke and Milton. It anticipates John Stuart Mill and the American Supreme Court Justices Oliver Wendell Holmes and Louis

A BILL *for establishing* RELIGIOUS FREEDOM, *printed for the consideration of the* PEOPLE.

WELL aware that the opinions and belief of men depend not on their own will, but follow involuntarily the evidence proposed to their minds; that Almighty God hath created the mind free, and manifested his supreme will that free it shall remain by making it altogether insusceptible of restraint; that all attempts to influence it by temporal punishments, or burthens, or by civil incapacitations, tend only to beget habits of hypocrisy and meanness, and are a departure from the plan of the holy author of our religion, who being lord both of body and mind, yet chose not to propagate it by coercions on either, as was in his Almighty power to do, but to extend it by its influence on reason alone; that the impious presumption of legislators and rulers, civil as well as ecclesiastical, who, being themselves but fallible and uninspired men, have assumed dominion over the faith of others, setting up their own opinions and modes of thinking as the only true and infallible, and as such endeavoring to impose them on others, hath established and maintained false religions over the greatest part of the world and through all time; That to compel a man to furnish contributions of money for the propagation of opinions which he disbelieves and abhors, is sinful and tyrannical; that even the forcing him to support this or that teacher of his own religious persuasion, is depriving him of the comfortable liberty of giving his contributions to the particular pastor whose morals he would make his pattern, and whose powers he feels most persuasive to righteousness; and is withdrawing from the ministry those temporary rewards, which proceeding from an approbation of their personal conduct, are an additional incitement to earnest and unremitting labours for the instruction of mankind; that our civil rights have no dependance on our religious opinions, any more than our opinions in physics or geometry; that therefore the proscribing any citizen as unworthy the public confidence by laying upon him an incapacity of being called to offices of trust and emolument, unless he profess or renounce this or that religious opinion, is depriving him injuriously of those privileges and advantages to which, in common with his fellow citizens, he has a natural right; that it tends also to corrupt the principles of that very religion it is meant to encourage, by bribing, with a monopoly of worldly honours and emoluments, those who will externally profess and conform to it; that though indeed these are criminal who do not withstand such temptation, yet neither are those innocent who lay the bait in their way; that the opinions of men are not the object of civil government, nor under its jurisdiction; that to suffer the civil magistrate to intrude his powers into the field of opinion and to restrain the profession or propagation of principles on supposition of their ill tendency is a dangerous falacy, which at once destroys all religious liberty, because he being of course judge of that tendency will make his opinions the rule of judgment, and approve or condemn the sentiments of others only as they shall square with or differ from his own; that it is time enough for the rightful purposes of civil government for its officers to interfere when principles break out into overt acts against peace and good order; and finally, that truth is great and will prevail if left to herself; that she is the proper and sufficient antagonist to error, and has nothing to fear from the conflict unless by human interposition disarmed of her natural weapons, free argument and debate; errors ceasing to be dangerous when it is permitted freely to contradict them.

    WE the General Assembly of Virginia do enact that no man shall be compelled to frequent or support any religious worship, place, or ministry whatsoever, nor shall be enforced, restrained, molested, or burthened in his body or goods, nor shall otherwise suffer, on account of his religious opinions or belief; but that all men shall be free to profess, and by argument to maintain, their opinions in matters of religion, and that the same shall in no wise diminish, enlarge, or affect their civil capacities.

    AND though we well know that this Assembly, elected by the people for the ordinary purposes of legislation only, have no power to restrain the acts of succeeding Assemblies, constituted with powers equal to our own, and that therefore to declare this act irrevocable would be of no effect in law; yet we are free to declare, and do declare, that the rights hereby asserted are of the natural rights of mankind, and that if any act shall be hereafter passed to repeal the present or to narrow its operation, such act will be an infringement of natural right.

This bill, drafted by Thomas Jefferson in 1777, first appeared "for the consideration of the people," in the form of a broadside similar to the above, printed in Williamsburg in the summer of 1779. The only known copy of the original broadside belongs to the Boston Public Library.

Brandeis. It applies not only to religion but to all the freedoms that are a part of the foundation of this nation.

It suggests the process of mutual persuasion that is the basis of a free society—a society in which there is no coercion of the human mind or human speech:

> *Truth is great and will prevail if left to herself; she is the proper and sufficient antagonist to error, and has nothing to fear from the conflict unless by human interposition disarmed of her natural weapons, free argument and debate; errors ceasing to be dangerous when it is permitted freely to contradict them.*

Capitol and Palace—June 1779

But the truth as Jefferson saw it did not prevail right away in Virginia. The General Assembly of 1779 declined to enact Jefferson's bill for religious freedom. Despite the atmosphere of Revolutionary ardor, the eloquence of the preamble, and the growing eminence of its author, the Assembly thought the bill went too far. And while Jefferson was in Virginia to observe this first presentation of his remarkable production before the public, observe was all he could do, because he was no longer a member of the House of Delegates.

Just before the committee's revision of the laws of Virginia was presented to the House of Delegates, Jefferson was elevated (if that is the word) to the governor's chair—the Assembly chose Jefferson governor and thus lifted him out of the legislative battle. His bill had to be presented by another member, and although it survived two readings it was then consigned to that limbo that legislatures reserve for those bills they are not quite ready exactly to reject, but do not want to pass, either.

The Revolution 1779–1783

Jefferson's bill remained on the table for a long time because the Assembly's actions, or nonactions, in the summer of 1779 in Williamsburg were the last such effort until after the fighting during the Revolutionary War ended.

The years immediately after the revisors' report were the years of active fighting in Virginia: a British raid on Portsmouth, the invasion of the state by Benedict Arnold, heavy fighting in the Carolinas, the invasion of Virginia from the south by a large British force under Cornwallis. These events understandably served to distract attention from issues of legal reform.

The fabled surrender of Cornwallis at Yorktown took place in October 1781, but technically the war lasted for almost another two years, with the British continuing to fight the colonists' ally France, and France's ally Spain, and with the diplomats scurrying across the water. The peace treaty between the Americans and the British was signed in Paris in September 1783 and was made known in Virginia in December.

Meanwhile, what of the chief author of those reforms stored up on the table by the interruption of the war? Life and history had forced upon Thomas Jefferson, too, some other preoccupations. His term as governor had not been happy, and his wife had died. After a year as one of Virginia's delegates to the Confederation Congress in Philadelphia, he left for Paris, where he was to serve as United States ambassador for five, on the whole happy, years.

It was up to his younger colleague, Jemmy Madison (thirty-four now, and sophisticated in the ways of government), to take over in the Virginia Assembly the fight for the Jefferson committee's revision of the laws of Virginia, including the bill for religious liberty. In the meantime, the Virginia government had moved from Williamsburg to Richmond, and the great days of Williamsburg's central place in Virginia history, and American history, were over.

Richmond 1784—Patrick Henry's Bill

Much had changed in Virginia during the war. Some church buildings were damaged. Religious observance had markedly declined. Back when Jefferson first criticized the established church, the General Assembly had temporarily suspended pay for the clergy, and it had never been reinstated; that had left many without a livelihood, and some had fled the country. Many of the Anglican priests—who had taken an oath to the king at their ordination—resisted the Revolution and fled to Canada or back to England. People felt public virtue had declined, and they wrote letters to the *Gazette* worrying about—as they put it—the spread of "Lewdness, Wickedness, and Vice."

Patrick Henry.

One of the most powerful people concerned about the state of religion and morality was Patrick Henry, the renowned orator and hero of the Revolution, a man both Madison and Jefferson had revered when they were younger. Henry had generally been regarded as a friend of the dissenters. He dressed simply, affected a common man's manner, associated with common people, played the fiddle, quoted no Greek or Latin authors. But Henry, along with others, believed that religion was necessary to morality, and that the morality of the populace was certainly necessary if this new kind of government, a republic, of the people and for the people, was to survive. And that led him to surprise many by taking the side usually favored by the conservative supporters of the old established church.

Henry introduced a bill called the General Assessment that provided for a tax to support "Christian teachers"—that is, pastors. The taxpayer would choose the denomination to which his money would be given, and those who made no choice of denomination would support the building of schools in their county. In this way it was more fair than the old laws which, under British rule, forced everyone to support the Anglican church. Some of Jefferson's lifelong friends argued ardently for this bill.

James Madison, on the other hand, was fully committed both to oppose what Henry and his group were proposing, and to support Jefferson's bill. One of his political maneuvers to those ends was to support Henry for governor—the Assembly chose the governor, a weak office then—in order, we presume, to get him and his eloquence out of the Assembly as the time came for decision.

Madison's Memorial and Remonstrance

Then, in the summer of 1785, on the advice of many people who were also writing petitions against the General Assessment, Madison wrote the now famous, but then anonymous, "Memorial and Remonstrance."

This is an eloquent, forceful petition stating why there should be no state-supported religion—even a religion in which the majority believes. It frames the argument with the republican principles that the patriots fought for, and at the beginning and the end it quotes the Virginia Declaration of Rights:

> *Religion or the duty which we owe to our creator and a matter of discharging it can be directed only by reason and conviction, not by force or violence. The religion then of every man must be left to the conviction and conscience of every man . . . this right is in its nature an unalienable right . . .*

Madison's "Memorial and Remonstrance" has been compared to the great libertarian writings of John Locke, John Milton, and Thomas Jefferson himself. Its force is such that the entire document has been reprinted as part of a United States Supreme Court Justice's opinion—not once but twice in the twentieth century.

Richmond 1785–1786—The Passage of the Virginia Statute for Religious Freedom

In 1785 there were so many petitions against Henry's General Assessment, including Madison's, that there was no fight. Under Madison's prodding the General Assembly took up, instead, the long list of revised laws for Virginia that Jefferson and his committee had written a long time before. Madison saw that the whole list of bills probably wouldn't be taken up, so he reached down through the others and plucked out the bill for religious freedom and brought it to the floor.

The debate was heavy, a few changes were made, and negotiations had to be carried on between the two houses. Finally, on January 16, 1786, the bill was passed. Jefferson's bill became the great Virginia Statute for Religious Freedom, one of the proudest accomplishments of his life.

Religious Liberty—and Otherwise—in the Other States

Virginia wasn't the only place where citizens were looking over the old laws. New constitutions up and down the eastern seaboard increased civil rights, decreased the power of the governor, created strong state legislatures. Eight states followed Virginia's lead and adopted a bill of rights.

What about religious freedom and disestablishment in these fledgling states?

In the New England states Congregational establishments inherited from the Puritan past would last longer than any others, well into the nineteenth century, but everywhere else there was rapid change. Many of the changes were influenced by the Virginia Declaration of Rights and the Virginia Statute for Religious Freedom.

Remnants of the established Church of England in several southern states—Georgia, North Carolina, and South Carolina—didn't last long.

Virginia, as we have seen, granted free exercise of religion in the June 1776 Declaration of Rights and the January 1786 Virginia Statute for Religious Freedom.

North Carolina was second only to Virginia in adopting, in the year of independence, a constitution guaranteeing religious freedom.

The 1777 Georgia constitution did insist that elected officials be Protestants (although they now omitted earlier derogatory references to "Papists"). In 1789, however, shortly after the Virginia Statute for Religious Freedom was passed, that constitution was amended to omit religious restrictions on anybody.

South Carolina's 1778 constitution provided for the establishment of the Protestant religion in excruciatingly specific detail; twelve years later that constitution, too, was changed to establish religious freedom "without discrimination or preference."

In the Middle Colonies there was a diverse pattern including considerable religious toleration.

In New York there was full religious freedom except for a requirement that naturalized citizens renounce foreign allegiance in ecclesiastical as well as civil matters—a requirement aimed at Roman Catholics. New Yorkers changed the word "toleration" to "free exercise" early in 1777 under the influence of Virginia's Declaration of Rights.

In Maryland, where the Catholic proprietor wanted both Protestant and Catholic residents, there had been an early act of toleration, liberal by the standards of the time; the toleration, however, had extended only to believers in the Trinity. When the leaders of the state wrote a new constitution in late fall 1776, they required Christian belief for the holding of civil office.

Pennsylvania, set up by the Quaker proprietor William Penn, never had an established church, although Quakers were dominant for some time. The state welcomed dissenters and sectarians of all kinds, and great numbers came from central Europe. At the time of the Revolution Pennsylvania did still require, for holding office, assent to the divine inspiration of the Bible, belief in heaven and hell, and a belief in one eternal God. Nevertheless, Pennsylvania's tradition of religious liberty and its early religious pluralism were very important in shaping the American tradition.

Delaware, with close ties to Pennsylvania, had a similar tradition of religious freedom. Its 1776 constitution required an oath of office to provide that the state would be governed by orthodox Christians. But in 1792 Delaware added a statement, clearly influenced by the Federal Constitution, prohibiting religious tests for officeholders.

New Jersey's 1776 constitution was fairly tolerant, although it excluded Roman Catholics from holding office until 1844.

Rhode Island had not sent delegates to the Constitutional Convention, and in this and other ways this small state had earned the disdain of the other colonies. Nevertheless, it had the earliest tradition of full religious freedom of any of the colonies and states—going back to its very origins, in the seventeenth century, with the great colonial leader Roger Williams.

Williams established Rhode Island, after his expulsion from Massachusetts, as a colony that insisted that there should be no civil disability whatever because of religious belief. He did this, not for eighteenth-century rationalist reasons, but almost uniquely in his time, for seventeenth-century Puritan Christian reasons.

Rhode Island came to be an asylum for dissenters and people with diverse religious positions of all kinds. It welcomed Quakers unwelcome in Massachusetts, and it became a haven for Jews in these overwhelmingly Christian colonies.

Vermont and Kentucky were not admitted to the Federal Union until after the Federal Constitution was adopted.

Vermont's 1782 constitution insisted that officeholders believe in "the Protestant religion." In 1791 this constitution was revised, omitting the required religious oath.

When Kentucky became a state in 1792, a bill guaranteeing religious freedom, written by Jefferson, was article three in their constitution. This Jeffersonian tradition continued in Kentucky for decades.

The Constitution—Philadelphia 1787

Meanwhile, the widespread dissatisfaction with the Articles of Confederation led the delegates to the Annapolis convention of 1786—prominently including Hamilton and Madison—to call for a further convention, ostensibly just to revise the articles, in May 1787. Delegates from—eventually—twelve of the thirteen colonies gathered in Philadelphia, the largest city in the colonies, where they proceeded to do much more than was expected. They produced, during that summer of 1787, the United States Constitution.

The delegation from Virginia was one of the earliest on the scene, and the most distinguished. The Virginians furnished, in the first place, the most revered figure in the colonies, General George Washington. The delegation also included James Madison, George Wythe, and George Mason, all of whom had, as we have seen, strong connections to Williamsburg, and the governor of the state, Edmund Randolph. Patrick Henry had been chosen but smelling a rat—as he put it—he declined to serve. After the convention he—and Mason—opposed ratification of the Constitution. Jefferson was in Paris representing the fledgling nation.

General Washington served as the president of the convention, lending to it and its product his indispensable prestige. James Madison was a principal figure—so much so that he has often been called "the father of the Constitution," although that is a term that he himself rejected.

The Constitution makers did not directly discuss the issue of religious liberty. In the document they wrote, however, there are several indications of the religious shape they expected the nation to take.

The body of the U. S. Constitution does not mention God, takes no religious position, makes no endorsement of Christianity or any other religion. It therefore is very different from—for example—the constitution of the modern state of Pakistan, which abounds in explicit references to Islam, and from many of the early state constitutions, which had references to Providence, to Almighty God, and even to more doctrinal beliefs in the Trinity or the authority of the Scriptures. The U. S. Constitution, produced in Philadelphia in the summer of 1787, had none of these. It showed that the new nation would not be a confessing state. Whatever religious affirmations would be made would be left to the voluntary choice of the citizens.

There was also no formal provision for the clergy or for an established church. To put it symbolically, there were no bishops in the U. S. Constitution—no Lords Spiritual in the House of Lords. That marked a break in the fourteen hundred-year history of Christendom.

George Washington.

In the one explicit reference to religion in the body of the Constitution, Article VI affirms that there should be no religious test for any office or public trust under these United States. That statement—very important in its own right—broke with the long and ugly history of requiring some religious profession on the part of people who would hold office in the states of European civilization. It also broke with the pattern of most of the American colonies, where there were provisions requiring belief in the Trinity, or in the Scriptures, or in God. But now, under the U. S. Constitution, there was to be no such religious test—by Constitutional prohibition!

Isaac Backus, the redoubtable Baptist leader, wondered whether he should lead his followers to support this new constitution; for two reasons he decided to support it. One reason was that there was no aristocracy—no Lords Spiritual or Temporal. And the other was that there was to be no religious test. (The Baptists rejected religious tests, and all use of state power in behalf of religion.)

When Jefferson's friends in Paris read this new Constitution, one can imagine that they thought it was an aggressive representation of their own skeptical, even hostile, views about religion. No confession of belief in God! No religious test! No bishops! It might have seemed to them that a great secular realization of their dream of a new order was coming into being across the Atlantic. But in a couple of ways the Constitution revealed that this was not so.

The writers of the French Constitution, a few years later, after the French Revolution, abolished the Sabbath—which of course is based on the Creation story in Genesis in which God rests on the seventh day—and substituted a ten-day week with a different kind of festival. They also abolished the Christian year and started numbering the years with the day after the autumnal equinox, when the Revolution had started.

The American Constitution did no such thing. In the context of a discussion of the President's response to bills passed by Congress—section seven of Article I—the writers mentioned a ten-day waiting period, and put in parenthesis (except Sunday). In other words, they, absentmindedly, if you will, took for granted the continuation of the Christian Sabbath.

And when they got to the end of the document, they dated the signing this way: "On the seventeenth day in September in the year of our Lord 1787 and of the Independence of the United States the twelfth . . ."

The United States was to be a mixture of a non-confessing legal order open to all religions and forcing belief on none, and a culture rooted firmly in the Christian heritage.

The First Amendment

The story of the founding of the nation did not end with the writing of the Constitution. The proposed Constitution had to be ratified by the states. Congress sent it to the state capitals, and in many of these there were close battles—particularly in Massachusetts, New York, and Virginia. Many old leaders—including George Mason and Patrick Henry in Virginia—insisted that the Constitution was flawed because it had no written guarantee of rights. Thomas Jefferson was writing from Paris that the document needed a bill of rights of the sort that Virginia had enacted first with its Declaration of Rights. Out of the politics of the ratification process came an agreement that after the Constitution was ratified, the pro-ratification forces would introduce a written bill of rights. In June 1791, in the first Congress, James Madison did exactly that. There was debate in the House and conference with the Senate, and then the proposed amendments were sent to the states to be ratified. When the process of adding the Bill of

James Madison.

Rights to the U. S. Constitution was completed in December 1791, religious freedom stood first in the list of guaranteed rights.

> *Congress shall make no law respecting an establishment of religion, or prohibiting the free exercise thereof.*

This was the first and the most fundamental of all the blessings of liberty that the founding fathers secured to themselves and to their posterity.

The Ending of State Establishments

Early in the nineteenth century the few remaining state establishments were ended.

In New Hampshire the Congregational Church was disestablished in 1817.

In Connecticut there was a Congregational standing order, an established state church supported by state power and taxation. It would last until 1818—supported by the Federalists, but opposed by the Jeffersonians, who included many evangelicals. The victory of the Jeffersonians in the elections of that year spelled the doom of the old standing order.

In Massachusetts the constitution of 1790, which John Adams had helped to write, provided for a kind of local option on tax-supported churches—tax-paid teachers of "piety and virtue." This system lasted until 1833—the last "establishment" of any kind in the United States, and by then an anachronism.

By that time Americans had come to share a common national belief on this subject. When the Frenchman Alexis de Tocqueville toured the United States in the 1830s, preparing to write his now classic study of *Democracy in America,* he discovered that everyone—including members of the Roman Catholic Church, even its priests—"attributed the peaceful dominion of religion in their country mainly to the separation of church and state."

Fifty years later the next greatest foreign observer of American institutions, the English ambassador James Bryce, in a widely known book *The American Commonwealth* published in 1888, wrote:

> *It is accepted as an axiom by all Americans that the civil power ought to be not only neutral and impartial as between different forms of faith, but ought to leave these matters entirely on one side,*

regarding them no more than it regards the artistic or literary pursuits of the citizens. There seem to be no two opinions on this subject in the United States.

Some Effects of Religious Liberty

What then actually happened in the story of religion in America? Thomas Jefferson predicted that by fifty years from the founding, the nation would be primarily Unitarian. Isaac Backus, the great Baptist leader, at about the same time made a different prediction: that within fifty years the nation would be overwhelmingly Baptist. And while these two were misfiring in this spectacular way, the president of Yale, Ezra Stiles, made what one would presume to be a more scholarly and disinterested prediction. He said that within a hundred years the nation would be about equally divided between the three religious groups, Congregational, Presbyterian, and Episcopalian.

All three predictions were proved to be wrong, although perhaps one could say Backus was a little less wrong than the others. In the first half of the nineteenth century, the Methodists and Baptists, the denominations of the common man and the frontier, grew rapidly in numbers and influence to become the largest Protestant denominations. An entirely new group, the Disciples of Christ, created on the American frontier, soon became a major religious community. From schism and from renewal, from argument and from new birth, a wide variety of religious communities grew from the lively experiment in religious liberty. Two other new religious groups, distinctive to America, with third scriptures of their own, arose out of the ferment of nineteenth-century religious pluralism: The Church of Jesus Christ of Latter Day Saints (Mormons) and the First Church of Christ Scientist (Christian Scientists.)

But the story of the development under America's system of religious liberty was not confined to developments within this country, or within Protestant Christianity. James Madison had defended the voluntary principle because it made the New World an asylum to the persecuted and oppressed of all nations. All of the religions of Europe came to the United States. Into this once most Protestant of countries there came, especially after the potato famine in Ireland in 1848, enough Roman Catholic immigrants to make that church the largest single religious body in the land. And into this most "Christian" nation, there came toward the end of the nineteenth century a Jewish population large enough to make the Jewish community in America the largest anywhere in the world until the founding of modern Israel.

The concept of religious liberty is closely tied to the concept of freedom of the mind. Though few now realize it, it was in the battle over religious liberty that the concepts of the free press and free speech were born, and in that struggle the underlying moral theory was developed. Insofar as the United States has realized those other great freedoms, they owe something to the heritage of religious liberty.

A Modern Affirmation of Freedom of the Mind

A case decided by the U. S. Supreme Court in the middle of World War II captures the essence of the American tradition of religious liberty and freedom of the mind.

An earlier opinion had held that schoolchildren who were Jehovah's Witnesses could be compelled to salute the flag even though their religion forbade it.

But in 1943 the court changed its mind.

Justice Robert Jackson, expressing the new majority opinion, wrote that a West Virginia statute making compulsory the salute to the American flag in the state's public schools was unconstitutional. That law, wrote Jackson, "Invades the sphere of intellect and spirit which it is the purpose of the First Amendment to reserve from all official control":

Compulsory unification of opinion achieves only the unanimity of the graveyard.

Justice Jackson gave a brief statement of the essence of American government:

We set up government by consent of the governed and the Bill of Rights denies those in power any legal opportunity to coerce that consent.

Authority here is controlled by public opinion, not public opinion by authority.

Thomas Jefferson would surely have approved Justice Jackson's sweeping summary:

If there is any fixed star in our constitutional constellation it is that no official, high or petty, can prescribe what shall be orthodox in politics, nationalism, religion, or other matters of opinion, or force citizens to confess by word or act their faith therein. If there are any circumstances which permit an exception, they do not now occur to us.

The United Nations, 1948, and the World

George Mason's Virginia Declaration of Rights, Jefferson's Virginia Statute for Religious Freedom, the Declaration of Independence, and the First Amendment to the Constitution have had worldwide influence. The indispensable ideas that they expressed, which were nurtured and debated here in Williamsburg—among them the belief in freedom of thought and of religion as the most fundamental human rights—have been a central part of the modern struggle for a better world.

During the first century and a quarter of this nation's existence, liberals and democrats around the world could believe that those ideas were coming to prevail worldwide. Throughout the nineteenth century, and until the First World War, the humane idea that governments and societies should respect the minds of their citizens gained ground.

But then came the dark events of the twentieth century.

The great political journalist George Orwell, considering the dark possibilities of totalitarianism and modern mass manipulation, wrote: "It is quite possible that we are descending into an age in which two and two will make five if the leader says so . . ." He went on to echo a great phrase from Jefferson but in a distressing way: "One has only to think of the sinister possibilities of the radio, state controlled education and so forth to realize that 'the truth is great and will prevail' is more a prayer than an axiom."

Orwell wrote this in 1939, before the full extent of the program of the Nazis was known, or that of the Stalinists fully understood, or the distinct features of totalitarianism clearly identified. He wrote it before the development, in Jefferson's own country, of commercial television, of sophisticated psychological marketing, of the domination of public discourse by "the engineers of consent." Preserving liberty of the mind, under which truth has a fighting chance, would seem to require of us now more than ever the eternal vigilance Jefferson mentioned in another connection.

George Mason.

Formal support for that liberty has widened. In the hopeful days just after World War II, as part of the process that created the United Nations, the nations of the world developed the Universal Declaration of Human Rights. This proclamation by the United Nations General Assembly became the most recent in that sequence of documents which began with Mason's Virginia Declaration. It was seen as a movement toward an "international bill of human rights" that would have not only moral but also, some day, legal force.

Three decades later, in 1976, that Universal Declaration was incorporated into three significant international agreements: the International Covenant on Economic, Social, and Cultural Rights; the International Covenant on Civil and Political Rights; and an Optional Protocol to the latter covenant.

Two of the provisions of the Universal Declaration of Human Rights deal with religious liberty in terms that echo the conversations held and the declarations passed or initiated in Williamsburg two centuries earlier:

Article 18
Everyone has the right to freedom of thought, conscience and religion; this right includes freedom to change his religion or belief, and freedom, either alone or in community with others, and in public or private, to manifest his religion or belief in teaching, practice, worship and observance.

Article 19
Everyone has the right to freedom of opinion and expression; this right includes freedom to hold opinions without interference and to seek, receive and impart information and ideas through any media and regardless of frontiers.

In large segments of the globe these principles are observed only in the whispered aspirations of peoples, not in the open actions of the powerful; they are, to quote Orwell, more of a prayer than an axiom. There is nevertheless value in stating the ideal, and making clear the principle, even where—perhaps especially where—it is not realized or observed. Making the ideal clear to ourselves is a step toward its realization. That is what George Mason and James Madison did more than two centuries ago here in Williamsburg, and what Jefferson did when on his little mountain to the west he wrote the words first presented to the world here in Virginia's eighteenth-century capital: "Truth is great and will prevail."

FIRST TEN AMENDMENTS TO THE U. S. CONSTITUTION

THE BILL OF RIGHTS

AMENDMENT I

Congress shall make no law respecting an establishment of religion, or prohibiting the free exercise thereof; or abridging the freedom of speech, or of the press; or the right of the people peaceably to assemble, and to petition the government for a redress of grievances.

AMENDMENT II

A well regulated militia being necessary to the security of a free state, the right of the people to keep and bear arms shall not be infringed.

AMENDMENT III

No soldier shall, in time of peace be quartered in any house, without the consent of the owner, nor in time of war, but in a manner to be prescribed by law.

AMENDMENT IV

The right of the people to be secure in their persons, houses, papers, and effects, against unreasonable searches and seizures, shall not be violated, and no warrants shall issue, but upon probable cause, supported by oath or affirmation, and particularly describing the place to be searched, and the persons or things to be seized.

AMENDMENT V

No person shall be held to answer for a capital, or otherwise infamous crime, unless on a presentment or indictment of a grand jury, except in cases arising in the land or naval forces, or in the militia, when in actual service in time of war or public danger; nor shall any person be subject for the same offense to be twice put in jeopardy of life or limb; nor shall be compelled in any criminal case to be a witness against himself, nor be deprived of life, liberty, or property, without due process of law; nor shall private property be taken for public use, without just compensation.

AMENDMENT VI

In all criminal prosecutions, the accused shall enjoy the right to a speedy and public trial, by an impartial jury of the state and district wherein the crime shall have been committed, which district shall have been previously ascertained by law, and to be informed of the nature and cause of the accusation; to be confronted with the witnesses against him; to have compulsory process for obtaining witnesses in his favor, and to have the assistance of counsel for his defense.

AMENDMENT VII

In suits at common law, where the value in controversy shall exceed twenty dollars, the right of trial by jury shall be preserved, and no fact tried by a jury shall be otherwise re-examined in any court of the United States than according to the rules of the common law.

AMENDMENT VIII

Excessive bail shall not be required, nor excessive fines imposed, nor cruel and unusual punishments inflicted.

AMENDMENT IX

The enumeration in the Constitution of certain rights shall not be construed to deny or disparage others retained by the people.

AMENDMENT X

The powers not delegated to the United States by the Constitution, nor prohibited by it to the states, are reserved to the states respectively, or to the people.

George Mason, Protector of Human Rights

Born in 1725, George Mason was a brilliant, impatient, and ailing man who was reluctant to leave his responsibilities at elegant Gunston Hall but was persuaded, because of "the necessity of the times," to become involved in the politics that had so much to do with the formation of our nation. Although Mason was not a lawyer, his legal knowledge and wise counsel were respected throughout the Virginia colony. Among those who very much respected, and learned from, this member of an older generation were Thomas Jefferson and James Madison.

Mason was the main author of the Virginia Constitution, a member of the House of Burgesses, a delegate to the Continental Congress, and—despite being a slave owner—a lifelong fighter for abolition. But his most important contribution to the nation took place when he wrote the Virginia Declaration of Rights. The Virginia Declaration of Rights, created in Williamsburg in May 1776, was written by a committee of which Mason was the head, and in Mason's hand. This document was the herald of a new social order when men's human rights and liberties would form the basis of government. Mason's declaration influenced the formation of governments both large and small: state constitutions took inspiration from it, the French Declaration of the Rights of Man was influenced by it, and Thomas Jefferson knew it well when—two months later—he wrote our nation's Declaration of Independence.

Years later, when he was sixty-two, at the Constitutional Convention in Philadelphia in 1787, Mason was a major contributor to the discussions about the creation of our Constitution. He wrote a major portion of the Oath of Office of the President, worked on the creation of the House of Representatives, and argued eloquently against increased importation of slaves. His major contribution to that document, however, was that he insisted that it should have a Bill of Rights attached to it. Without such a document, stating explicitly the duties of government to its citizens, Mason felt, the new nation could turn back into a monarchy, or at least "a corrupt and oppressive aristocracy." He refused to sign the Constitution without such a Bill of Rights.

He carried on the battle in the Virginia convention considering whether to ratify the bill-less Constitution. Out of these arguments a compromise was reached: the Constitution was ratified, but its proponents—prominently including James Madison—promised to introduce a Bill of Rights in the first Congress, which Madison did. In considerable part through Mason's efforts, the bill was added to the Constitution in 1791.

Mason died at Gunston Hall in 1792. Few Americans who have served their country as brilliantly have met with as little recognition. Every citizen who cherishes his freedom should be grateful to George Mason, that reluctant statesman.

The Great Little Madison

James Madison, who was to play such a central role in creating the tradition of religious liberty in our country, was a small, slight, reserved, sickly, and bookish man who signed his name James Madison, Jr., until he was well into his fifties. Born in 1751 to an Anglican planter in the Piedmont's Orange County, he was sent as a young man to the College of New Jersey at Princeton, a stronghold of Presbyterian dissent, where he was infused with the exciting atmosphere of the Scottish Enlightenment and acquired a decided sympathy for religious dissenters.

Back in Virginia after graduation, ill and missing his college days, he had an experience that transformed his sympathy into political action. Visiting the jail on a trip to Culpeper County, he found a group of Baptist preachers imprisoned for voicing their religious sentiments. Madison was shocked: these men had been doing no more than his Presbyterian colleagues at Princeton had done! He wrote to a friend to "pray for liberty and conscience to revive among us," and spoke up for the Baptists, quickly becoming known as a friend of dissenters.

Thus began his long and remarkable career in the political life of our country. He played an important part in each of the four deciding points in making our tradition of religious liberty: first, in 1776, he amended the article on religion in the Virginia Declaration of Rights to assert the equal right of every human being to free exercise of religious conscience; second, he composed the most pungent of all American documents on this subject, his 1785 "Memorial and Remonstrance against Religious Assessments"; third, he resurrected Jefferson's draft of the Virginia Statute for Religious Freedom and steered it into law in 1786; and finally, he proposed and drafted the first amendments to the Constitution that were to become the Bill of Rights, in which the very first clause of the First Amendment deals with freedom of religion.

Madison's devotion to his country was admirable and long-lasting: he read, wrote, and thought about government continually, and held public office almost without a break from his twenty-third year until he retired from the presidency in 1817, when he was sixty-six. About Madison's contribution to the tradition of religious freedom in this country Canon Stokes has said, "He should be remembered with gratitude by every earnest Jew, Catholic, Protestant, and member of every other sect in the United States."

"Almighty God hath created the mind free . . ."
                                              Thomas Jefferson.

Credits

PORTRAITS: *Thomas Jefferson,* by Gilbert Stuart, Colonial Williamsburg Collection. *George Wythe,* twentieth-century copy by William H. Crossman, Colonial Williamsburg Collection. *Patrick Henry,* by Thomas Sully, Colonial Williamsburg Collection. *George Washington,* by Charles Willson Peale, Colonial Williamsburg Collection. *James Madison,* by Gilbert Stuart, Colonial Williamsburg Collection. *George Mason,* by D. W. Boudet, 1811 (after a lost painting by John Hesselius), courtesy of the Virginia Museum of Fine Arts, Richmond, gift of David K. E. Bruce.

DOCUMENTS: *Fry-Jefferson Map,* Colonial Williamsburg Collection. *Virginia Declaration of Rights,* Virginia State Library and Archives. *Virginia Statute for Religious Freedom,* Colonial Williamsburg.

HISTORIC BUILDINGS: By Colonial Williamsburg photographers.

This publication has been made possible through the generosity of Mutual of America.